HOW TO TALK TO YOUR
CHILDREN
ABOUT DIVORCE

Understanding What Your Children
May Think, Feel, and Need

✂

JILL JONES-SODERMAN
MSW

ALLISON QUATTROCCHI
DIVORCE MEDIATOR, ATTORNEY

❧ PREFACE ☙

Most people going through a divorce are overwhelmed by the process and the issues. Although there are many books on divorce available, they are often wordy, too inclusive, and too overwhelming for a person who is struggling with the emotional ramifications of a divorce. This series of short books gives the reader the ability to choose the information he or she needs and to get valuable knowledge on that subject in a quick and easy manner. The understanding and awareness these books can bring to the divorcing individual will contribute to that individual's ability to better manage his or her divorce. They are a real bonus for the divorcing public and for professionals who work with divorcing clients.

❧ ACKNOWLEDGMENTS ☙

To the many people who have contributed their knowledge, support, and encouragement to this project, and to those who have written or are writing for this project, I offer my heartfelt thanks. Special thanks to Sheila Steinberg, my editor, without whom this series of books would have been almost impossible.

– Allison Quattrocchi, J.D.
Family Mediation Center Publishing Co., LLC
Co-author and Publisher

CONTENTS

❧ INTRODUCTION ❧

The bond of love, attachment, and caring between each parent and his or her children is the means through which children are socialized into becoming functioning adults. This bond has a life and integrity of its own and manifests differently with each child. When parents divorce, a child's life is shaken. And, at a time when the parents are most distraught, they must also heighten their awareness of their children's vulnerability. A tall order. Paying attention to the child's thoughts, feelings, understanding, and behavior, however, is critical to protecting the bond between each parent and each child and to protecting that child's ability to adjust in the healthiest way to the change in his or her circumstances. **Whatever each parent says at this time will be indelibly etched into the child's memory.**

The goal is for parents to provide the support and nurturing necessary that allows the child to come away from his or her experience of the divorce with the basic underlying feeling that the parents tried to do the best they could—to be there, to care, to respect the child's feelings. This kind of support will enable the child to deal with the aftermath of emotions that pour forth when that child learns of his or her parents' plan to divorce.

The authors take it for granted that you want to raise emotionally healthy, well-socialized children, and that you do not want your divorce to impede that goal. With concern for your children, and sensitivity to the difficult emotional and practical challenges you may be facing at the time of your divorce, the authors offer the best guidance they can for protecting your children. This information will be most effective if both you and your spouse are able to read it as partners in parenting. The authors assume you are not faced with such specialized traumatic issues as domestic violence, child abuse, and addiction. These complex issues need to be addressed in a different framework.

How can parents help their children cope with the decision to divorce and continue to promote their children's healthy emotional development?

⚜ I: THE CHILDREN WE ALL ASPIRE TO RAISE ⚜

■ The Vision

Each parent has a vision about the type of person his or her child will become. The bond between child and parent reinforces and sustains that vision through all the challenges and complexities of child rearing. Because divorce can temporarily interrupt that commitment as the parent becomes overwhelmed by his or her own emotional rollercoaster, it is appropriate to review the elements of character that most of us strive to encourage in our children.

Courage. Ability to be confident enough so he or she can think, explore, try, fail and try again, and be able to see failure as an opportunity for new learning.

Self-Esteem. Ability to sustain a self-image that is separate and unassailable from the images others have of the child. A child wants to feel capable and strong.

Responsibility. Ability to accept praise or blame for actions or choices the child makes and to carry out the roles expected of him or her as a member of the family and of society.

Stability. Ability to hold consistent feelings and images of others because of a history of nurturing and trust.

Capability to Love and to Honor Commitments. Ability to care about others, to sustain emotional attachments, and to be empathetic.

Judgment. Ability to make choices that allows the child to survive, be successful, and thrive in the world.

In sum, we want to raise children to become independent, caring, and self-sufficient adults who are good family members and good citizens.

■ The Divorce and the Vision

> ## A Child's Wish
> A seven-year-old boy, when asked by his counselor what his three wishes were regarding his parents' divorce, replied, "I only need one wish—for my parents to be friends."

Divorce is an event that must be dealt with and overcome so that the vision you have for your child can be sustained and realized. It is important to remember that the divorce itself will not destroy your child's life. The harm will come from the extent to which you allow yourself to be negatively affected by the challenges created by the divorce—challenges to your goals, your values, your vision for the future, and your attitude toward life. The harm will be increased by the duration and intensity of the conflict between you and your spouse. A high level of conflict produces:

- Parental interpersonal hostility that engulfs the child;
- Loss of focus on the child's feelings, ideas, and needs for stability;
- Loss or lessening of the strong emotional bond between the child and *each* parent;
- Interference with the flow of communication between you and your spouse; and
- Decreased ability for each parent to be a positive role model.

Accepting the loss of the marriage in a more positive light than you might be inclined at the moment may help to diminish the duration and the intensity of the conflict. Your children can provide you the opportunity to give a unique meaning and purpose to the parenting relationship outside of your own loss, expectations, and disappointment—if you will allow it.

Your behavior and that of your spouse in this situation are also the models that will guide your children's relationships to both of you, their siblings and friends, authority figures, and their own interpersonal relationships in the future. Although it may be overwhelming to accept this responsibility at the time of the divorce, you must give it your best shot. Your children are depending on you.

ⅩⅤ II: PREPARING TO TELL THE CHILDREN ⅩⅤ

Planning to tell the children about the decision to divorce is an opportunity to set the stage for how you and your spouse will relate in your new roles as parents after divorce. How you proceed will probably be a reflection of whether you make life decisions thoughtfully, impulsively, or avoid them altogether.

■ Children's Personality Styles

Your child's personality style affects your child's adjustment and reaction to the divorce and how you, the parent, react to the child. Parenting is a dynamic interactive process. Children have character styles and personalities that elicit different feelings and responses from the parent. A parent may respond differently, for example, to a timid, shy child than to an aggressive, bold child. Parents may discourage one style and encourage the other.

A child who is flexible, calm, and easygoing may cause a parent less concern when anticipating talking to him or her about a plan to divorce than an assertive child with strong attitudes and opinions. The assertive child may need to have advanced warning about the meeting to discuss the decision to divorce and to be coached on how he or she can be most helpful. This child may take over, not allow others to speak, be directive, and opinionated. He or she needs to be encouraged to let any other children participate and respond. A child who is shy and sensitive has difficulty with change and feels embarrassed easily. The shy child needs time to think and adjust to the idea of a significant change.

■ Think Through the Issues

The process of thinking through and planning for what, when, and where to tell the children about your plan to divorce begins with your personal insight and visualization of how to set the stage for this purpose. With your spouse, if possible, think through the issues you see as potential problems for both of you. Share your fears about telling the children with your spouse and listen to any concerns he or she might express. Then, practice.

Telling the children cannot be used as a stage for self-pity, blame, martyrdom, or an opportunity to align the children for or against either parent, other members of the family, or significant others.

Begin by asking yourself the following questions that will help you prepare for the event: Have you enough self-awareness and enough self-control that you can focus on the needs and feelings of the children? Can you be attentive, provide appropriate interaction with the children, and respond to their requests and reactions? Can you and your spouse brainstorm about what some of their reactions might be and agree on appropriate responses? Do you each respect each child's bond with each parent? Do you both understand the fact that a child's feelings, no matter what they are, must be honored?

Ideally, your answers are all "yes," but the need here is for honesty and you may have to answer "no" to some of these questions. If so, perhaps that will show you where you are less prepared. The best-case scenario may be that your increased awareness will empower you to stop yourself when you sense you are acting or responding in opposition to any of these goals. If you are unable to do any of this processing because you are too emotionally embroiled with your spouse or too overwhelmed by your life circumstances, you might consider having your children stay temporarily with other trusted adults who can provide more stability for them in order to shield them from the immediate fallout. When children get assaulted by their parents' emotional conflicts, they may manifest rebellious or helpless behavior as a means of trying to get their own feelings attended to.

■ Practice Damage Control

What your child hears about your plan to divorce, your child will remember forever! The thoughtful parent will be conscious of the memories he or she is embedding for the child and do his or her best to make those memories as constructive as possible.

1. What Not to Do

A parent's attempt to influence, manipulate, control, or distort a child's understanding or view of events will come back to haunt that parent. Such attempts at manipulation most commonly manifest in downgrading and blaming the other parent. If you are so inclined, remember that when you blame and complain about your spouse, you are jeopardizing your child's self-image. Your child sees himself or herself as a part of each parent. Typically, he or she loves the other parent, may look like the other parent, admire qualities in the other parent, or share characteristics of the other parent. Any antagonism you display toward that other parent will be perceived by your child as a sign that you feel the same antagonism toward him or her.

When you engage in attempts to manipulate and control your child's view of the other parent or the divorce, you are also teaching your child to use these same techniques—techniques that can later be used against you and others. Trying to manipulate or control your child may also teach your child not to think for himself or herself. As a result, your child may be inclined to having his or her own thought processes overpowered by others. Such a child can become a confused and dysfunctional human being.

At some point in his or her life, your child will become aware of having been manipulated or overpowered and his or her resentment toward the culpable parent is likely to be enormous.

Your child's resentment over the time lost with the wronged parent will often be accompanied by feelings of grief, disillusionment, betrayal, and lack of trust toward the manipulative parent. On the other hand, if left to his or her own resources, your child will eventually sort out the reality and come to an understanding of the role each parent played in the divorce. This is the best strategy.

When you tear down the other parent, you might as well be tearing down your own child.

Another behavior to avoid is making promises you cannot keep. When there is a divorce, parents are often tempted to address their guilt by trying to "make it up to the child" and make promises they cannot deliver. For your child, the broken promise is a form of abandonment that undermines his or her inherent joy of anticipation with the now-present expectation of disappointment. This can permanently affect his or her view of life and create a tendency toward pessimism and lack of trust.

2. What to Do

Your goal as a parent is to help your child deal with his or her feelings and to adjust in a way that allows your child to see beyond the moment. Despite the hostility you and your spouse may harbor toward each other, these feelings must be set aside so you both can present a united front in support of your child and provide an emotional safety net. The level of communication between you and your spouse and your ability to work together are critical to the overall adjustment of your child at all stages of your divorce. The history of your relationship with your child—the level of trust he or she has in your love and the sense of security already established in the family—will affect how well the reality will be accepted by him or her. Remember the following:

In general, your child will do as well as you do. Your goal is to put together the best post-divorce family you can. Your child, no matter what age, will pick up on emotions—your sadness, happiness, tension, and the like. Your behavior concerning the divorce may affect your child's mental health for years, as well as his or her future relationships with significant others. So, check yourself.

As parents, you need to treat each other with respect. This is the biggest gift you can give your child at this time. Own that each parent has faults and also good qualities and try to emphasize the latter. Perhaps you will need to draw on pleasant memories of your spouse rather than focus on the present situation.

Your child will go through the same grieving process you go through. Respect your child's grief and be understanding. This may require an extraordinary effort on your part at a time when you are also dealing with your own grief. However, it is not fair to your child if you quit, even momentarily, being a parent.

You are your child's most significant role model. Continue to be a teacher for your child by setting the best example you can. This is a good time to model for your child a constructive approach to conflict resolution and to teach him or her that change is a part of life and can mean growth and opportunity.

Be as upbeat as possible about the change and the future. If you can, give your children some assurance about where they will live and go to school, or, if you cannot make assurances, tell them what your goals are in that respect.

■ Be Aware of Negative Feelings

Divorce often triggers negative feelings and reactions that interfere with a parent's ability to express genuine feelings and support for his or her child. Those feelings also interfere with the parents' ability to work together as partners in parenting. Being aware of these feelings and reactions is part of the preparation for telling your child about the divorce. Getting help to work through these feelings as quickly as possible is the best way to get them under control, put them behind you as quickly as possible, and enhance your role as a supportive parent. Be alert for the following reactions, as they can sabotage any family meeting you have for the purpose of preparing your child for the divorce:

Vengeance. It is easy when you are in pain to want to seek vengeance toward the person you perceive has hurt you. Vengeance is an extreme response and, as a reader of this book, you probably either have not reached this level or you have gotten this feeling under control.

Anger and Blame. As with vengeance, pain gives rise to anger and anger to blame. Anger may manifest on the part of one or both parents toward each other and can cycle through feelings of disappointment, to extreme displeasure, to hostility, and to rage.

Fear. Fears often arise around the contemplation of divorce, as change may lead to a sense of impending danger and vulnerability.

Guilt. If you are the spouse who initiated the decision to divorce, you may be feeling a sense of having done something wrong. If you are not the spouse who initiated the divorce, you may be blaming yourself for some action you did that you feel caused the other spouse to decide to divorce. Or, you may feel a sense of guilt or self-recrimination because of your societal, family, or religious expectations that may generally disapprove of divorce.

Pessimism. Divorce does not usually leave anyone feeling upbeat in the short term. More likely, divorce can inspire feelings of negativity that can cause one to sink into depression.

The goal is to be aware of any of these tendencies and to confront them in a way that reduces the damage each can cause to your relationship with your child and your spouse. Realize that each of these reactions is common. Then realize they are temporary. Lastly, adjust your mindset and get the help you need that will allow you to put your negative reactions into perspective and move on. These feelings do not have to be imposed on your child or your spouse. (Booklet no. 4, "**Taking Control of Your Divorce**," discusses constructive approaches to getting control of these reactions.)

Awareness of the slightest tendency toward any of these reactions may be enough to give you the courage to keep them under control when talking with your child or your spouse. Such awareness may also allow you to participate meaningfully in a cooperative divorce process, such as mediation or collaborative divorce. (Booklet no. 2, "Other Ways to Get a Divorce," explains these processes.)

⚛ III: TELLING THE CHILDREN ⚛

Breaking the news about the decision to divorce is usually a traumatic and sad event. Many children are not aware that dissension between parents may result in the end of the relationship. They may never have known the relationship to have been any other way, so it may seem to them that dissension is how men and women relate. Some children may know that their parents are not getting along well and fear that separation or divorce may be near. This fear is constantly feeding a sense of insecurity in them. In these cases, actual knowledge of the divorce may even provide some relief and a confirmation of what they already know. Nonetheless, the actual event of telling the children is extraordinarily distressing for almost all children.

Your deepest concern must be to minimize circumstances that perpetuate harmful memories around the announcement of the decision to divorce.

■ When to Tell the Children

1. *Timing Issues for You and Your Spouse:*

• Make sure the decision to divorce is irrevocable for you or your spouse before telling the children. Despite the regrets, sadness, and wishes that the divorce was not happening, one or both of you have taken or are about to take steps to proceed with the divorce, and you each can acknowledge that changes in the present situation will soon be made.

• You need to give the news to the children before you give it out to other family members, friends, or neighbors. In this way, you are more in control of what your children hear and your children have some time to prepare to meet the reactions of others to the news.

• Ideally, telling your children will coincide with a time when both you and your spouse have come close to accepting the divorce, have some life plans in place, have begun to entertain a constructive view of the future for yourselves and your children, and when each of you is capable of focusing on the emotional needs of your children. If you can achieve all this before it is imperative that the children know that a divorce is contemplated, you will have achieved a bit of a miracle.

• Balance all this, however, with the fact that children are amazingly intuitive. They often suspect trouble before parents do. If arguing or tension is constantly present, many children will have already expressed some fear about a divorce. You are doing a disservice to your children by not telling them the truth. To keep them wondering about what is happening is to contribute to their insecurity, anxiety, and fear.

• Tell the children as calmly as possible and at a calm time.

• Unless the animosity between you and your spouse presents too great a risk, it would be better to tell the children together.

2. *The Worst Timing for Children:*

• Avoid breaking the news to children on special days like birthdays, anniversaries, holidays, or any other date that is of particular importance to them, for it will forever spoil that special event.

• Avoid breaking the news around events that are important to the child, such as school plays, games, special play dates, or the beginning of the school year. It is important to keep your child's life, activities, and interests as intact as possible.

• Avoid telling the children before bedtime, as this will interfere with their ability to sleep and may create ongoing sleep problems as the news of the divorce becomes associated with going to bed.

• Avoid telling children in a public place, such as a restaurant, where they are unable to react comfortably and naturally.

• Avoid telling children in a place where they cannot withdraw from the family to seek privacy or comfort from a trusted confidante. Often children do not want to deal with either parent at this time.

• Avoid telling the children when they are ill or otherwise physically vulnerable.

• And, as has been mentioned previously, avoid telling children about plans to divorce when you (or you and your spouse if you are telling them together) are in an emotional state that might prevent you from responding to the children's feelings and needs. Perhaps it will be helpful to remember that a child cannot handle your grief on top of his or her own.

Children are empowered by their ability to communicate. The ability to communicate becomes meaningful when adults respond to the child with effective communication and show respect for the child's communication. Particularly at this time, being available and able to answer your children's questions is critical.

In sum, the best laid plans will allow your children the greatest latitude of expression, privacy, and ability to reach out to whomever they trust the most and feel can provide them with the most comfort.

There is never a perfect time to tell the children, but there are better times.

■ **Dealing with Adult Emotions in the Presence of Your Children**

Although you can be expected to be emotionally distraught in the presence of your children, boundaries about what you say to them are critical. Certainly you can share your overall sadness about the divorce, but stay away from the details. Denial or minimization of your feelings, your children's feelings, or the situation does not help your children learn how to deal with their emotions. In these circumstances, you can provide some balance by talking about what you plan to do to feel better and to move on.

Allow your children to be comforting. But, boundaries are critical here as well. You can help your children see themselves as a source of comfort to you, but not as gatekeepers for the flow of information, or as caregivers, or as the orchestrators of your life or anyone else's. They are not capable of parenting you nor should they be expected to.

Have patience. It is important not to put words in your children's mouths because you are rushed or annoyed. Do not tell them what to think as they will learn to disregard you, just as you, by telling them what to think, will have disregarded them. Do not make your point by saying, "You are just like . . ." or "Why can't you be just like . . .?" or indignantly stating, "What were you thinking?" "What was going on?" or "Why did that happen?" Assuming that you understand why your children did or said something is the best way to ruin communication—long term and short term. Ask for an explanation in a gentle way and without making assumptions. It is humiliating and diminishing to your children's self-images to have motives attributed to them that are incorrect.

Children typically love both parents. Do not place your children in an impossible situation by asking them where they want to live or any personal questions about the comings and goings of your spouse or how the children feel about your spouse. This places them "between a rock and a hard place." They cannot say much very comfortably without being concerned about hurting their other parent. Alternatively, in an attempt to secure a parent's approval, children, particularly those who feel extremely insecure, may skew information to please a parent. Children have sensitive antenna and often are aware of what a parent wants to hear—then they oblige.

A Child's Story

David, who was eight and one-half years old, was caught in his own loyalty conflict with his parents. He did not want to declare a position on his residency for fear of possibly hurting a parent's feelings. He wanted everything to be fair. When asked by a counselor what he would wish for in answer to his dilemma, he responded, "I wish I could go inside a copy machine and make a copy of myself so Mom and Dad could each have one of me."

This story illustrates the reason why most child therapists do not recommend that you ask your child with whom he or she wants to live. It is agonizing for your child to be placed in that position. There is nothing wrong with considering your child's wishes, but a counselor or therapist is the best person to determine your child's preference.

■ What to Tell the Children

Some of the suggestions for what to say to your children depend on the age of the child or your own special circumstances. The children should be together during the initial discussion, but talks with each child afterwards may be helpful.

Children can take in only so much information at one time. For young children, one-half hour or less on average is enough time for the first disclosure. Notice if the child becomes distracted or tries to change the subject. Pick the most important points from below, follow the child's lead, and set another time for further discussion if you sense he or she cannot take any more.

1. Messages Children Need to Hear:

Do not hesitate to adapt the messages your children need to hear to your situation and your words. Make sure those adaptations are neutral, geared toward what your children can absorb, and are tailored to their needs—not yours.

• Depending on the age of your children, you may want to explore with them what their understanding is of the word "divorce." Some will have friends whose parents have divorced. They may have some peculiar notions and some fears about divorce. If you can, you might point out a healthy divorced family situation so the children can feel some relief. Young children may attribute the cause of the divorce to an imaginative fantasy figure. Clarify for them any misunderstandings they may have, but also be realistic about the situation.

A Child's Story

Seven-year-old Sharon was asked what it means when her mother said she and Daddy were getting divorced. Sharon answered with absolute certainty, "You go to the judge and he says, 'Are you sure this is what you really want?' You say, 'Yes!' You give each other a kiss, then the judge takes your rings away!"

- Do not indulge in long explanations. Children do not need involved reasons or fancy language. Forget words like "incompatible," "psychological or sociological factors," "philosophical differences." Explaining the meaning of divorce may be as simple as saying "Daddy and Mommy have decided not to live together any more. We are getting divorced, which means we will no longer be married."

- Be careful about overindulging the "why." Children do not need to hear about the girlfriend or boyfriend, or any other behavior that puts blame on a parent, no matter how indignant, sad, mad, or betrayed you feel. Keep it simple and say something like the following:

"We are sorry but we feel this is what needs to happen."

"We loved each other when we were married but have grown apart.

"Although we care about each other, we can no longer live together."

"This is not what we intended to happen when we were married."

"We are not doing this to make things worse, but to make things better."

"We know you would like us to stay together but we cannot remain together and be happy."

"We know it hurts you to hear this."

"Mommy and Daddy are not perfect. We both have made mistakes. We are sorry."

"We have thought about it for a long time. It was not an easy decision."

These suggestions assume both parents accept the need for the divorce.

Some Children's Views of Why their Parents are Divorcing

1. David, three and one-half years old, was asked why his parents got divorced. His reply: "Because my mother was not a very good cook."

2. Another child reported his father said he was sick and tired of his mother's headaches.

3. "My mother is older than my father is and my father said he will only play with people his own age. They were the same age when they got married, but my mother says my father is always such a child."

4. After four-year-old George spent the day with his father, they went to a restaurant for dinner. George picked up his father's cell phone, which was lying on the table, and pushed the button for his mother's cell phone. When his mother picked up the phone, George said "You're late. We're waiting for you for dinner," then looked at his father and said, "No wonder you're divorcing her."

A Child's Story

Two sisters, five and one-half years old and eight years old respectively, were talking about their parents divorce and seemed rather bouncy and unfazed by it. Another child, whose parents had a stormy divorce, asked, "Aren't you sad?" The younger sister replied, "You get divorced so you can date, go out to dinner, kiss in the car, plan the party—'wedding,' corrected the older sister—and we all get new dresses, except for Daddy. He has to wear a tie." (Divorce appears to have been romanticized by someone for this little one.)

2. *When One Parent Does Not Want the Divorce*

When one parent does not want the divorce, the situation is even more painful for that parent and telling the children often becomes emotionally more difficult. This also raises an issue about what to tell the children about who made the decision to divorce. Certainly, if you are the reluctant parent, you are not required to present a happy face or to represent to the children that you and your spouse are in agreement. Honesty is the only policy—but not coupled with judgments and blame or elaborated with too much information or inappropriate information. Try something like, "Your (father/mother) has come to the conclusion (he/she) cannot be happy in the marriage and has asked for a divorce. I do not want this but there is no point in staying in a marriage when one person wants to leave."

No matter how miserable you feel, do not be pitiful, dependent, self-righteous, or blaming. Your children cannot handle that on top of their own grief, nor should they ever have to. And remember, insulting your spouse is a direct attack on your children's self-worth. The initiator of the divorce may have to be prepared for being cast as the "bad guy" for a while, but the truth is hard to hide. The children's tendency to blame when there is an initiator may result in more pain for the initiator and short-term damage to their relationship with that parent. However, if both you and your spouse accept the fact there were reasons in the marriage that did not make the situation happy for the initiator, the children may avoid this damage.

Affairs are probably the most common catalyst for divorce—but affairs are symptoms, not causes. Do not blame the divorce on the affair. Many other reasons can contribute to a spouse's no longer wanting to stay in a marriage. Some of the more extreme issues, such as alcoholism, sexual problems, homosexuality, drug usage, domestic violence, or personality disorders, are more difficult to explain to children appropriately, but some explanation is advised. Lack of truthfulness or hiding of information will only contribute to the children's distrust of you and your spouse. Some of these issues may not have been present when you married, were present and were not important or not obvious to you at that time, or worsened over the years. Alternatively, you may have been filled with the optimism of your love, and you hoped the person would change and the issue would go away. Perhaps one of these reasons is the only explanation you can offer your child. Again, too much of "why" may be as negative as no explanation at all.

You might want to discuss what to say about these type of issues with a therapist or counselor before speaking with your child.

3. The Biggest Fears for Children

The biggest fears for children when there is a divorce are around losing a parent or being responsible in some way for the divorce. They desperately need to hear reassurances from the parents like:

"You are part of both of us."

"We are not doing this because you have done anything wrong."

"We are unhappy with each other, not with you."

"You are our joy and the gift of our relationship."

"We both love you and always will." (Children cannot hear this enough.)

"We are not divorcing you."

"We are still your Mommy and Daddy."

"We will be your parents forever."

"Neither of us is going to leave you." (If this is true.)

"You will spend time with each of us." (Explain living arrangements if you know what they will be or what you are contemplating. Let your children know you want those arrangements to work for everyone, including them.)

"This is about our problems and has nothing to do with you. You did not make this happen."

"You don't have to choose between us."

"You could not have prevented the divorce."

"We will do our best to always provide you with the loving support and stability you want and need."

"We will still be a family, just a different kind of family."

It is important that children realize that at the time of their birth, their parents loved one another and that they were "wanted children." This will help them realize they were not the reason for the divorce.

A Child's Story

Jimmy was nine years old. He had been asked to come to the mediator's office to talk with the mediator alone about any of his concerns regarding his parents' divorce and what he would like to see happen regarding the arrangement for parenting time with each parent. In the process of talking, he remarked how scared he had been when his father moved out of the house a year ago. As he recalled the memory, his face fell, his whole body crumpled, and in a frightened and haunting voice, he whispered, "I thought he was gone forever." The mediator, shaken by the boy's demeanor and obvious pain, asked, "How long was he gone?" "Four days," he answered.

It is wise to remember that a child's sense of time is not that of an adult. An absent parent needs to recognize this and contact his or her children frequently to let them know that the absent parent cares, is okay, and is still there for them. Without this contact, it is easy for the children to blame themselves for the divorce.

A Child's Story

Five-year-old Jamie pleaded with God in her bedtime prayer. "Please, God, I love both my parents so much. Are you going to take them away from me because I have been such a bad girl and I don't deserve them?"

4. Keep the Children Out of the Fray

Give your children permission to stay out of any emotional chaos between you and your spouse:

"You don't have to take sides with either one of us."

"We want you to feel free to love both of us."

"It is a difficult and emotional time for us; we may have some arguments, but this is an adult issue and you never have to feel that you need to take care of either of us. It is not your responsibility. It is our responsibility."

"We will try not to put you in the position of taking sides, but if we slip up, please remind us that we told you that you do not need to get involved or take sides."

"Our emotions may get the better of us now and then. If either of us says anything to you or asks you a question about the other that makes you feel uncomfortable, feel free to tell us you are feeling (upset, uncomfortable, frustrated) by the comment or question. You have our permission to remind us not to put you in the middle."

"Tell us how you really feel. We want to know. We promise we will listen to you and will try to help you the best we can." (Only promise if you know you can set your own grief aside and really listen.)

Do not put your children in the middle or let them put themselves in the middle. Your divorce is your problem. Do not make your children part of your problem.

A Child's Story

Things were a little raw at the Hansen home. The agreement about how their son, Greg, was going to go back and forth between each parent's home was not going well. The mediator asked the parents to bring ten-year-old Greg into the office, so she could see what Greg might want to say about the situation. Fortunately, his parents were wise enough and trusted the mediator enough to allow Greg this opportunity, even knowing some things he might say might not be flattering. During Greg's meeting with the mediator, Greg begged the mediator to tell his parents to "PLEASE STOP using me to pass messages back and forth between them. I feel like my father has one arm and my mother the other and they're tearing me apart."

There was no doubt that Greg was feeling a tremendous amount of anguish.

This is a common issue and it is a cruel role to thrust on the child. Parents do it unwittingly because of their own pain, as their concerns for their own needs overshadow their ability to understand what they are doing to their child. Had they given Greg permission at the time of telling him about the divorce to speak freely to them if he felt they were making their problem his, he might have been able to deal with it sooner. But children want to please and help their parents, so it is very easy for them to get caught in the middle between their parents, especially in a divorce situation.

Another common complaint children have is when a parent quizzes them about what they did or with whom when the child was under the other parent's care. Unless this truly stems from a safety concern, the questioning parent is out of line.

A Child's Story

A five-year-old boy, whose parents were constantly fighting, was asked where he wanted to live. He replied, "By myself on the moon." For him, escaping the parental discord made the moon a rather attractive place to be.

A Child's Story

The parents of five-year-old Grace, a rather precocious child, were divorcing and it was the holidays. Mother said to Grace, "I'm so sorry your dad and I are not together for the holidays." Grace responded, "I can handle the divorce, you just need to suck it up."

Mother had never said the word "divorce" to Grace. Grace was obviously more aware of what was going on than her parents thought and she did not want to be reminded of her mother's sadness about the divorce.

---

5. Reinforce Your Child's Support System

You and your spouse, your child's friends, siblings, relatives, teachers, and maybe even some of your friends may be part of your child's support system. Allow your child to seek support wherever he or she wishes. Sometimes a child feels more secure with one parent than the other. This is no time to be jealous of your child's bonding with anyone else, including your spouse. Give your child permission to share by saying something like "It's okay to tell your friends. It's not a secret." Or, "You may feel upset and confused and have feelings such as sadness, fear, guilt, hurt, or anger. You don't have to keep your feelings to yourself; you may talk with either of us (or other trusted adult) about how you are feeling if you want to." Ask about your child's feelings. But do not be surprised if your child is hesitant to share them with you. Your child loves both parents and is often afraid of saying something that could hurt one or the other.

Tell your child, "We will always be ready to listen to any questions you have." Answer your child's questions the best you can. If you don't know, say so, but assure the child that when you have the answer, you will let him or her know. If the question touches on a subject that is too personal, you might say, "There are certain things that Mommy and Daddy consider personal. We will do our best to answer your questions, but please also respect our choice not to answer if we feel that sharing the information does not meet our need for privacy or our need to protect you from having to deal with adult issues."

Siblings are also an important resource for a child. Expect and encourage your children to share their feelings with each other.

❧ IV: AGE-RELATED DEVELOPMENTAL ISSUES ❧

■ General Comments for Children of All Ages

It is often difficult to know whether the child's behavior is a normal reaction to a disturbing situation such as divorce, whether the behavior indicates the child is abnormally stressed by the situation, or whether the behavior has a physical rather than an emotional cause. If your child's stress is overwhelming and support for him or her is not adequate, you may see the child regressing to earlier stages where he or she was more comfortable and secure. To assess your child's stress level, ask yourself the following:

• Are there changes in more than one area of functioning (for example, temperament, language, interaction with other children) that persist for more than two to three days?

• Are the behaviors severe?

• How prolonged are the behaviors?

• Is there improvement or deterioration in those behaviors once there is recognition of the behaviors on the part of the adults and that recognition has been followed by some form of intervention?

To help you to better understand normal and unusual behaviors and to respond appropriately to them, a discussion follows that addresses the developmental goals, symptoms of stress, and interventions that are specific to children of different age groups.

■ Infants to Children Two Years of Age

The developmental goal for babies is to thrive—to eat well, sleep comfortably, move their bowels without constipation or diarrhea, have their diapers changed and enjoy bathing and, finally, to gradually express recognition and pleasure at the presence of the baby's caregivers and significant others.

One looks for the infant to enjoy physical touch, to mold into the arms of the person who holds and cuddles him or her, to feel comforted and soothed when cuddled, to laugh, gurgle, be active in exploring the world through touch, sight, oral incorporation, and to respond to voices of known figures by eye and body movement. Babies who stiffen their bodies when one reaches to hold them or babies who do not know how to be held will react like sacks of potatoes when being lifted. These are children at risk for attachment disorders.

When babies are continually upset in response to noise, change of routine, tension and anxiety, one can expect disturbances in all the later stages of development. Crying, crankiness, proneness to colds, fevers, and asthmatic reactions are typical of babies who feel stressed. Babies who feel exceptionally stressed cry excessively, have difficulty being comforted, vomit, and appear inconsolable. A baby becomes distressed around fighting, an atmosphere of tension, and a disorganized routine. When calm and peace are restored, the baby becomes normally active and reactive. These stress reactions must be differentiated from colic, gastrointestinal disorders, or complications in breast feeding, such as when a breast-feeding mother under stress is not lactating and the baby is not being fed.

Interventions:

• Consult your pediatrician to evaluate basic medical health;

• Maintain a stable, nonviolent, calm emotional atmosphere. Feeding, bathing, diaper-changing, and toilet training are all opportunities for nurturing.

• Maintain stable and consistent caregivers and a stable routine.

• Maintain a level of physical contact and stimulation.

■ Children from the "Terrible Two's" to Five Years of Age

The central developmental tasks of this stage of childhood have to do with the development of trust, attachment to parents, beginnings of a sense of rules and of right and wrong, self-assertiveness, the power of thoughts and words, and empathy. Children are not able to be assertive, exploratory, and sensitive without the pleasure they receive from the reinforcement and approval of their parents. Children are more likely to give up one behavior for another not out of fear, threats, or punishment but in response to love and approval.

Our children's ability to model behaviors that make us proud of them and make them capable of handling themselves when they are away from us is largely based on what they see. For this age child, language development mixes reality and fantasy, as words create a new power base for understanding and managing the world. Dreams, cartoons, and television may be just another level of life and are real to the child. This age child cannot differentiate in the abstract. For instance, a four-year old on the phone with his father might hold up a picture for his father to see, saying, "See what I made for you."

Young children either feel magically responsible for a divorce or magically in control. Their defense against their sense of total lack of control may be that they believe there are magical strangers in the world who are luring loving parents away from each other and their children, as the songs of the Sirens in Greek mythology lured sailors into destructive seas.

A Child's Story

One four-year old burst into tears when her mother was caressing the family dog. The child was at once angry and upset. When asked why she was having such a reaction, she responded, "You love the dog more than Daddy. If you put Daddy out, am I the next to go?"

A child whose parents are at war may have unpredictable contact with one or both parents, irregular schedules, inconsistent caregivers, and generally be exposed to chaos and neglect. When children are neglected and their role models fail to model, children do as they please, guided by impulse and pleasure. Adherence to rules and healthy social conformity are met with hostility and disregard.

Regressive behavior is a common response to stress and confusion. Children in this age group who have been toilet trained suddenly have many accidents; bedwetting that ceased may reappear; sleeping through the night alone in the child's own bed is replaced with nightmares and a need to sleep with the parent. A child who was cooperative may become demanding and generally out of control in an effort to exert his or her will over the parent. Children who feel poorly attended to will be angry, aggressive, uncaring, and unwilling to share.

Crying is a clear symptom that follows. Does a child cry to get something he or she wants in response to conflict around the child or to conflict with another child? Do tears of frustration follow criticism? Is crying an avoidance tactic or a bid for attention? Does the child cry in the morning? This may indicate that the stress of the new day is too much to bear. Or, is the child tearful or moody at the end of the day when hungry or having to go to bed alone?

When crying becomes sobbing or inconsolable sadness—unremitting after the child has been given comfort or the desired object—the parent must look at this symptom as going beyond the bounds of a normal reaction to changed circumstances and look more closely at the situation in which the child is living or review the child's medical history for further evaluation. The understanding and sensitivity with which one deals with an upset child will teach empathy and understanding or indifference and cruelty. Time and attention at this stage can help the parent as well as the child avoid therapy and legal fees later.

Although it is preferable for parents to be consistent in their parenting techniques and rules, fighting with your spouse about changing his or her parenting style rarely works and basically serves to remind you why you got or are getting divorced in the first place. If possible, both of you should seek professional help in achieving more parenting consistency.

Interventions:

• Take the time to understand what your child is reacting to, feeling, and trying to say. Even with children this young, help them to discuss and reason through these reactions. Try to discover the source.

• Attempt to separate reality and fantasy, but remember that the journey from full-fantasy thinking to substantially reality-based thinking has just begun, and your effort may be met with inconsistent comprehension on the part of your child.

• If your child is crying to manipulate the situation or seek attention, do not make eye contact with him or her and continue your activities until the child stops crying. Then try to find out what the crying was about and talk about why this behavior is unacceptable.

• If a child is throwing tantrums in public, respond by removing the child to a private place. Understand that this is the child's attempt to exert control and create order and sense out of feelings of loss and helplessness.

■ Children Ages Six to Twelve

The developmental tasks of the pre-teen years have to do with establishing reality-based and abstract thinking—that is, thoughts around home, family, loyalty, and friends. The sense of community and participation in school all become real concepts in time and space. Morality (right and wrong) takes on real meaning and is related to consequences. Children in this age group are beginning to see themselves both as others view them and with regard to their own idealized sense of self. They identify themselves with their mothers and fathers, but know they are also different. They recognize their talents, have a sense of goals and aspirations, or have none and feel lost.

Children in this age group often feel extremely alone and shaken when facing the prospect of the dissolution of the family. Life appears unpredictable. "Who can be counted on?" the child might feel. All that the child held to be true, safe, and sound is now questioned and the child might think, "If my parents no longer love each other, will they fall out of love with me?" Relatives whom the child once took for granted as part of the family are now seen as having loyalties to one parent and as having either negative or undefined loyalties to the child or the child's other parent.

A Child's Story

A seven-year old was invited to a family event with her father, who was in the midst of divorcing her mother. The child eagerly looked forward to the family event until her mother reminded the child that her father's brother, her uncle, played a humiliating joke on the child at a prior family event and that her mother would not be there this time to intervene. The child would not have recognized the uncle's inappropriate act if the mother had not made an issue of it. The mother, however, insisted that, if the child were to attend, the child needed to check in with her periodically because she questioned father's ability to be adequately attuned to the potential behavior of his brother. The good feeling that first surrounded the thought of going to a family party became shrouded in ambivalence and anxiety. The child declined to go and then was upset about not going, which in turn upset the mother.

(Continued on page 32)

(*Continued from page 31*)

The point is that when one parent interferes with the thoughts and feelings of the child, there will be consequences to that parent that would not have been there if the child were allowed, instead, to arrive at his or her own decision. The opportunity for the child to act with a certain amount of independence and fearlessness has been tarnished. Teach children to be thoughtful, aware, and alert to problems or potential problems. Give them coping skills to deal effectively with feelings of insecurity so they may handle a given situation and not feel immobilized.

When life has become more complicated than expected, as in the case of a divorce, crying and feeling overwhelmed and frightened are typical behaviors of a child of any age. Schoolwork may be affected as these feelings result in restlessness, poor concentration, and counter-productive beliefs, such as, "Who needs to worry about school when my whole world is falling apart?"

Interventions:

• Help the child to articulate in his or her own words (not yours) what he or she is thinking or responding to. For example: "Sweetheart, what do you hear me saying to you"? or "Say back to me what you understand me to have said."

• Teach the child to describe things and events accurately. For example: By this stage of development, names for body parts and functions such as "vagina," "penis," "feces," "urine," and "anus" need to be understood as a clear expression of physiology. Pet names can create confusion and misunderstanding. This can become critical when parents are mistrustful of each other, as is often the case in a divorce.

A Child's Story

A child who stated that her Daddy put his "pee pee" in her "wee wee" created a child abuse investigation because of the adult misunderstandings around those words. Ultimately what was discovered was that the child meant that her father had urinated in the toilet where she urinated and did not flush the toilet. The thought she was trying to express was that both her urine and her father's mixed together in the toilet.

■ Children Ages Twelve to Seventeen

Adolescence is often described as a time of self-absorption, rebellion, and distancing from the family with a sense of disapproval and embarrassment. Peer relations rule as replacements for family authority and control. This oversimplification of the adolescent, yet soon-to-be adult, identity discounts the reality of the adolescent as a combination of both parents.

The adolescent is now an individual with a sense of self and how the surrounding world works. In early childhood, the child's self-image is a reflection of the parents, whom the child, in most cases, adores. The adolescent's self-image is a mix of many images, including his or her own image of what he or she wants to become. Significant among these images are the most prominent characteristics of both parents. The adolescent will adopt the reality of the same-sex parent and the idealized self-image that parent unconsciously projects. From the parent of the opposite sex, the adolescent will learn what is admired and emulate those characteristics as well. For example, boys want to be like the men their mother's admire. In general, the adolescent also incorporates aspects of the role models their parents admire or disdain, depending somewhat on the attitude of the adolescent toward his or her parent.

All these images create a repertoire of models for identification and creativity in trying out new roles. These roles are played out in the adolescent's world at home, at school, with peers, and in the world of work. Adolescence is the time of trial, an individual's effort to set boundaries as he or she chooses from this repertoire of images to eventually find self-identity.

Most of all, the task of the adolescent is about the exploration of the world—the courage to go out, to do new things, to find one's own path, and to return home to share what he or she has learned for affirmation, support, and guidance. Divorce and family disruption interfere with the adolescent's need for self-focus and the freedom to explore and solidify his or her own identity. To protect these needs, which are akin to self-preservation, adolescents will often stick their heads in the sand when circumstances occur that might demand attention away from their own lives. Divorce is such a circumstance. This behavior in response to a divorce is not unusual for a young adult who is focused on defining his or her personal goals and sense of self.

Interventions:

• Adolescents tend to withdraw or to be explosively angry at the news of the family disruption—the "this-is-the-last-thing-I-need-right-now" reaction. The adolescent's need may be to run from the offending parents to friends, who offer a haven of stability. If such a sanctuary exists that you approve of, be glad. Your child is probably in good hands and will return to family integration once he or she feels that his or her life plans, school, and goals are still intact. Then your adolescent will talk to you. This reaction is a moderate retreat from the parents. Your job is to be a loving, supportive, non-critical presence.

• This same response can occur to a greater extreme. The adolescent totally retreats from adults and withdraws to close ranks with friends—ones you may not approve of—and maybe even runs away. These adolescents are harder to reach. They need to be wooed and entreated into contact so that a strong family bond can be established or reestablished. Often professional help is needed for this bond to occur.

• The tendency of adolescents to react to divorce with extreme emotion (anger, serious depression, or withdrawal) requires that you be alert and ready to actively intervene. You need to understand what the adolescent is responding to, what he or she thinks is going on and fears might happen in the future. It is critical to find out quickly as adolescents are mobile and have access to cars, peers, alcohol, and drugs as quick solutions to painful situations. Respectful discussion of events is a discussion not from parent to child but from parent to young adult who has his or her own definite ideas.

• The young adult often fears abandonment and replacement. As much as young adults want to "be free," they are not quite ready and grudgingly and probably unknowingly rely very significantly on the security of their home base. A divorcing or divorced parent may be preoccupied with his or her own needs—the possibilities of new liaisons, new directions, and more career demands. These and other changes in the parent's life threaten what was once a normal routine for that parent and the young adult. Maintain respectful distance, absolute availability to talk, poised vigilance, and attentiveness to school performance, choice of friends, and the overall relationship with you, your spouse, and other family members.

The parental goal is to establish rapport, mutual respect, and to keep the adolescent focused on his or her life and goals.

A Child's Story

Fourteen-year-old George was part of a family discussion of his parent's plan to divorce. The parents assured the children that their lives and best interests would be of the highest priority and that things would remain essentially unchanged regarding living circumstances, schools, and the like.

Shortly after the discussion, George went to dinner with his parents, wanting very much to have time alone with them. He asked his parents questions about when they knew how they felt, when they made this decision, and the possibility of reconciliation. The parents answered the questions to the best of their ability. However, throughout the conversation, the parents continued to snipe at one another. At a particularly contentious moment, George bitterly exclaimed, "Just whose interests are you looking out for now?" In other words, George wanted, needed, and expected the focus to be on him and felt abandoned by his parents continual fighting with each other.

❧ V: THE INFLUENCE OF BIRTH ORDER ❧

The birth order of children within a family affects their behaviors, personalities, and general characteristics. It may affect what the child needs to hear about the divorce and his or her responses to it.

■ The First-Born Child

The first-born child tends to identify strongly with his or her parents and authority figures in general. More pressure is often put on these children to live up to the family ideal and to be role models for younger children. The parents' hopes, dreams, and wishes tend to be well-formulated for the first child. As a result, the responsibility and expectations placed on that child are often overwhelming for the child. The consequences for the first born, if he or she cannot realize the family's expectations, may be devastating.

If one parent has left the home and is not present as often as that parent had been, the first-born child is inclined to feel he or she must fill in for that parent and may take on the roles of parent to siblings and protector to the remaining parent. Often the remaining parent is seduced into relying on the oldest child for emotional support, parenting, and child care. Because divorce intensifies these responses, the oldest child can be in danger of losing his or her childhood to a parent's adult dependency needs. This is a destructive pattern, and parents need to be forewarned to be on the lookout for their own behavioral patterns that could contribute to it.

In any case, it is especially important to let the first-born child know that he or she does not have the responsibility of caring for the other parent, that the divorce is an adult problem, and that it is the adults who must deal with it. Give the child permission to tell each parent to please not use him or her as a sounding board, a confidante, or a go-between, or involve him or her in the issues, financial or otherwise, of the divorce.

A Child's Story

Five-year-old Nancy said to her Mother, "Now, when you talk to Daddy, make sure you are nice, speak in a sweet voice, don't make him a dump truck."

You have to wonder what kind of interactions she observed between her parents that prompted a response that was so protective of her father.

■ The Middle Child

The position of middle child (or children) refers to a span of less than six years between that child and the older and younger siblings. The middle child may lack the status of the older child and may not receive the parental attention given the youngest child. The concern for the middle child is that older and younger siblings have a way of staking out territories and establishing their place in the family. The tendency then is to find some personal characteristic with which to brand the middle child, such as "Smarty," "Clown," "Neatnik," and the like. This can narrow the middle child's self-image. These children may also feel somewhat impoverished emotionally, as if they have not gotten their share of attention.

Fear of feeling ill-defined, superfluous, devoid of any meaningful family role may cause the middle child to seek out peers for affirmation. Where peer group support is valued as a place of comfort, middle children tend to develop early independence, self-sufficiency, and sophisticated peer group skills. A primary concern for middle children is their sense of uncertainty as to their position in the family and their definition of self.

Parents need to support this child's tendency to seek support outside the home and encourage the child to express his or her feelings and thoughts. Pay particular attention to bolstering his or her self-image and making sure this child understands he or she had nothing to do with the reason for the divorce. All children need to hear this, but the middle child is more vulnerable to having this concern than the first born or the youngest child.

■ The Youngest Child

The youngest child is often considered the most pampered and likely to have received preferential treatment and attention from the older children and the parents. The youngest child is always playing catch-up as everyone else has knowledge and competence that he or she has yet to attain. Sometimes this leads to a sense of isolation. The youngest child's options are to have everyone else attend to his or her needs or to learn independently all that the child needs to know. The race to catch up to everyone else is a primary motivating factor for the youngest child. This, however, can cause the child to abandon projects out of fear of not being good enough.

In a divorce situation especially, youngest children are often worried about who is going to take care of them and if there will be adequate resources left. They may also worry about being left behind or separated from their siblings. Sibling support needs to be encouraged. The truth is that life for this child will be different than it was for the older children and this child will spend more time than his or her siblings in the post-divorce family. This may impact both the child's relationship with his or her siblings as well as with each parent—for better or worse.

■ The Only Child

In the formative years, the only child does not experience the conventional sibling rivalry that occurs when there are other children. This child never has to share parental praise or compete for the attention of a parent, neither does this child experience the routine insults and criticisms of siblings. For this reason, the only child is often extremely sensitive to criticism. This child may also see one parent as a competitor for attention from the other parent. It is also common for parents of an only child to be overly protective and intensely involved with the child, sometimes even to the extent of interfering with the development of adequate peer relations.

The only child usually relates well to adults and is more awkward with his or her peers. As children, they tend to be most privy to adult information, may be more aware of the controversies within the household, and feel more responsible for them. Thus, this child may more easily feel he or she is to blame for a divorce and suffer more than children who have siblings. Feelings of abandonment are more likely because of the only child's dependency on the parents. Although all children may worry about the parent who has left the home, the only child may have even more of a tendency to do so.

These children are also especially vulnerable to parents who may use them as confidantes and explain more or expect more than the child can handle at his or her age, even though the child appears precociously mature. The parent who is inclined, particularly in times of trauma, to treat this child as a "best friend" or caretaker or predictor of outcomes is making a terrible mistake. These children often are in the position of having to choose one parent over the other or withdraw, are self-destructive and compromise their own development by not doing well or withdrawing from school. Avoid questions of your child like, "Do you think your father will send the support check?" "Do you think your father will remarry?" "Do you think your mother's boyfriend will move in with her?" "Do you think (the parent's new boyfriend or girlfriend) will call me?" These questions force an adult issue on the child and are not appropriate.

A Child's Story

Father routinely took his eleven-year-old son to visit his mistress because the mistress had two children who were the child's age and who attended the same school as the child. This created a situation in which the child's friendships with his peers were compromised. His allegiance to his mother was strengthened out of the protectiveness he felt toward her and the guilt he harbored about going to see father's mistress. His father chose to look at his child as though he were someone with whom he could share adult intimacies. The fact that the son saw himself as being used by the father to create an excuse to visit his mistress did not occur to the father and only came to the surface when the child lashed out at the father's mistress and called her a "whore." His eventual hostility toward his father destroyed the son's relationship with him.

A Child's Story

Jerry and Jane had a rocky marriage. A lot of arguing and dissension between them had been escalating over the last few years. When they decided to divorce, they fretted over telling their six-year-old daughter. They were anxious and kept putting it off because of fears of breaking down, worries about how she would react, and how to tell her. With the encouragement of their mediator, some practice with what they each would say, and other information they had been provided, they set a time when they would sit down with their daughter and tell her. Both of them were floored when their six-year-old daughter looked up at them and said, "All I want is for everyone to be happy." Obviously, even at six years old, she knew a lot more about them than they had ever dreamed she knew.

A Child's Story

1. Kaleigh is three years old and an only child. Her father has moved out of the family home. Kaleigh says, "I'm so proud of Daddy that he can sleep alone—but who is going to tuck him in at night?"

2. The first thing Marci, an only child who is six years old, did when she went to her father's house was to open the refrigerator. When asked why she did that, Marci replied, "I just want to be sure he has enough to eat."

❧ VI: CHILDREN'S SHORT-TERM REACTIONS TO DIVORCE ❧

Following is a general list of children's reactions to divorce that are usually short term and common:

• Expect a reaction—anger, sadness, and tears. Be patient.

• A child may be embarrassed and worry about what people will think. This can be especially true of teenagers.

• A child may be silent. Teenagers, in particular, worry about what will happen to them. Younger children may be inclined to worry about the welfare of one or both parents, particularly the parent who has left the house.

• A child may be scared of his or her own emotions.

• A young child may become very clingy out of fear of abandonment, especially if the child feels one parent has "left."

• Some children will over-perform and try to be perfect out of fear that if they are not, they may be abandoned.

• A child may act out his or her fear and anger or not be able to concentrate in school because of emotional confusion and increased insecurity. Patience, Patience, Patience! Get your child some help, if at all possible.

• A child may act out to get attention, as he or she may be getting the short end of the stick because of a parent who is too focused on his or her own emotional issues.

• A child may start to assume the role of the parent who has left the house.

• Denial is very common. Young children especially may be constantly expressing the hope or expectation that their parents will reconcile. A child may make suggestions overtly or covertly, trying to encourage interaction between the parents.

• Crying is a natural expression and helps release the tension and anxiety that the child feels. A greater concern is the child who represses his feelings as these feelings can later manifest in less healthy ways.

❧ VII: THE EFFECTS OF A "GOOD" OR "BAD" DIVORCE ❧

■ A "Good" Divorce

"Good" divorces, ones that are resolved in an atmosphere of cooperation that promotes emotional resolution, growth, and the ability to move on, produce children who adjust well to the divorce and also move on. This divorce is an event in the child's life that occurs between the parents. However, it allows the child to settle into a new routine with stability and order, and fosters the continued contact with both parents and the possibility of new routines and insights. In this situation, the child is ready to establish relationships with each parent that will evolve with the child's experience and maturity. There is, however, no divorce that does not affect a child. The only question is to what degree.

■ A "Bad" Divorce

If the divorce has been very rocky, perhaps even ugly, the risk is that the unhealthy dynamics between the parents will continue. For the child in this situation, the divorce becomes a lifestyle, not an event. This divorce may represent for the child the loss of one parent. Contrary to the loss of a parent due to death, when it is common for a child to idealize the parent, the loss of a parent due to divorce is usually cloaked in animosity and negative exaggerations of that parent's character or role as a parent. Divorces like these are often products of the adversarial process. The nature of that process increases, may even create, polarization and distortions of reality between the parents that engulf the child. The child becomes the repository of the effects of the emotional atmosphere that surrounded the divorce.

In families rife with conflict before, during, or after divorce, a child may try to become the peacemaker. Trying to soothe hostilities serves the child as a defense to his or her anxiety and sense of helplessness. Helplessness returns when the child's efforts are not met with success. This cycle may manifest in the child's having continuing fantasies and thoughts about the reconciliation of the family for many years, even when there is every indication to the contrary.

■ The Effect of "Good" and "Bad" Divorces on Communication

Children see things differently than adults. Communication for most adults is difficult enough without the added emotional complications of a divorce. If you have ever heard the same event reported by two different witnesses, you are well aware of how dramatically different the reports can be. Add to the mix the mind and viewpoint of a child and the results can be even more diverse. Parents forget this. When Mom and Dad each have two households, the indirect rather than direct involvement with each other contributes to more opportunity for misinformation passing between the households through the children. A parent's reliance on a child's version of what someone said or did, coupled with residual distrust from or during the divorce, and the reduced availability of the other parent with whom to verify the information often results in accusations or misunderstandings between the parents. These can create confusion or anger and add to the communication meltdown and general anxiety for everyone.

A "bad" divorce implies little or no constructive communication between the parents, and the resulting misunderstandings between the adults are hazardous enough to navigate. However, communications to one parent from a child, perhaps about events when the child was with the other parent or about what that parent said are especially vulnerable. The listener, who is usually the other parent, often immediately assumes the child's version is accurate. The listening parent's level of anger from the divorce may further feed the assumptions about the communication. The result is an angry parent, a misunderstood child placed in the middle, and the other parent unfairly accused of remarks that were misinterpreted. If you find yourself in this position, you must give the remark some latitude, not react, and try to verify what the child has said with the other parent. In a "bad" divorce, however, the reality is this clarification will not take place and the tension will escalate.

In a "good" divorce, where the conflict has, at a minimum, been managed more productively than that in a "bad" divorce, the parents are more likely to seek some clarification with the other parent about the child's communication. Thus, the likelihood of increased conflict over such communications between the parents is reduced.

A Child's Story

A seven-year-old child reports to his therapist: "I can't get all the stories straight. I asked Daddy for $32,000 and he asked me what it was for, and I told him, 'Roller skates. I think I was supposed to ask you for roller skates.' I can't remember whether I am supposed to say something or not supposed to say something."

This child is being used as a conduit between the parents and has been asked to relay information he does not understand and, in fact, has misunderstood. He is confused and frustrated.

Children deserve your best effort, especially during the most chaotic times of your life. It is during those times that your attention to the children will be more difficult for you to provide but more important for the children to receive. You are their beacon. You are their guide. Your choices can either wreak havoc in their lives or pose a challenge that changes their lives, may bring discomfort and pain, but does not devastate them. The authors hope the information in this book will assist you in supporting your children through the difficult period of your divorce and help everyone adjust to and function in a healthy way in your new post-divorce family.

❧ THE CHILDRENS' BILL OF RIGHTS ❧

1. The right to be treated as important human beings with unique feelings, ideas, and desires, and not as a source of argument between parents.

2. The right to a sense of security and belonging derived from a loving and nurturing environment that shelters them from harm.

3. The right to a continuing relationship with both parents and the freedom to receive love from and to express love for both parents without having to stifle that love because of fear of disapproval by the other parent.

4. The right to "listening parents."

5. The right to know and appreciate what is good in each parent without one parent degrading the other.

6. The right to grow and flourish in an atmosphere free of exploitation, abuse, and neglect.

7. The right to know that their parent's decision to divorce is not their responsibility and that they will still be able to live with each parent.

8. The right to have a relaxed, secure relationship with both parents without being placed in a position to manipulate one parent against the other.

9. The right to have parents who do not undermine time with the other parent by suggesting alternatives to the children or by threatening to withhold activities with the other parent as a punishment for the child's wrongdoing.

10. The right to be able to experience regular and consistent parental contact and the right to know the reason for not having regular contact.

11. The right to be a kid and to be insulated from the conflicts of the parents.

12. The right to be taught according to their development levels, to understand values, to assume responsibility for their actions, and to cope with the consequences of their choices.

13. The right to continuing care and guidance from both parents so that they can be educated in mind, nourished in spirit, and developed in body in an environment of unconditional love.

14. The right to honest answers to questions about changing family relationships.

15. The right to be able to participate in their own destiny.

16. The right to be able to view both of their parents as positive role models for their values and their behavior, including the demonstration by their parents of good conflict-resolution skills.

A list of other booklets that are available or that we will be publishing follows. We also plan to add others. Please check either of the following Web sites for additional titles. Orders may also be placed on either Web site.

www.divorceinanutshell.com

www.azfamilymediationcenter.com

OTHER HELPFUL BOOKLETS IN THIS SERIES

#1. How to Have a Successful Divorce
   Allison Quattrocchi, Divorce Mediator/Attorney
#2. Other Ways to Get a Divorce
   Allison Quattrocchi, Divorce Mediator/Attorney
#3. How to Talk to Your Children About Divorce
   Jill Jones-Soderman, MSW
   Allison Quattrocchi, Divorce Mediator/Attorney
#4. Taking Control of Your Divorce
   Allison Quattrocchi, Divorce Mediator/Attorney
#5. What You Need to Know About Health Insurance
   Michael J. Malasnik, Risk Specialist
#6. Divorce: How to Use Life Insurance
   to Protect Your Agreements
   John Pope, ChFC, Life Insurance Specialist
#7. Divorce and Your Money
   Marion Johnston, Chartered Financial Consultant
   Elizabeth Goff, CPA
#8. Dividing the Marital Home,
   Retirement Assets, & Debts
   Allison Quattrocchi, Divorce Mediator/Attorney
#9. Divorce: How to Protect Your Heirs and Your Assets
   Thomas Murphy, Estate Planning Attorney
#10. Purchasing or Refinancing Your Home
   Luanna Bayer, Mortgage Specialist

Excerpt from Booklet #1
"How to Have a Successful Divorce"
By Allison Quattrocchi, Divorce Mediator/Attorney

What can you bring to your divorce so it can occur with the least amount of emotional and financial damage to you and your family?

I. CHANGING THE VIEW

■ The Words

The words you use set the stage and have the power to create the play.

"Shame!" "Failure!" These words usually frame the initial reaction to the announcement of a divorce. Such words reflect our concerns about what our friends and family will think and the loss of hopes and dreams of what our lives were supposed to be. Cultural messages compound our sense of shame and failure. Your first positive step is to take control of that reaction and reframe it in words that are more thoughtful and caring. **Divorce is not a failure; it is a sadness.** When you change your view, you see differently.

■ Eliminating Any Need to Blame

Viewing divorce as failure can trigger the need to blame the other person and sometimes yourself for what has happened. Blame feeds anger and creates havoc for the divorcing parties and their children. **Anger clouds judgment!** Eliminate the need to blame; it only massages your ego and creates pain. Discourage your friends and family from indulging in blame. Offer them and yourself an explanation based only on divorce as a sad reality and invite them to be supportive in a helpful way.

■ Embracing the Concept of a Successful Divorce

The concept of a successful divorce is as important as the concept of a successful marriage.

Making a commitment in the beginning to the concept of a successful divorce is your choice. This choice will foster a more positive attitude, which, in turn, will improve your experience and your outcome. After all, attitude is the only thing over which you have total control. Your challenge is to move forward and not stay mired in what might have happened or should have been. No one promised you life would be fair. We all have some personal history we can choose to perceive as "unfair." It may well be unfair, but staying stuck there will only keep you stuck there. Jon Kabot-Zinn captured this concept in the title of his book, *Wherever You Go, There You Are.*

■ Taking Responsibility for Your Own Happiness

The truth is that seldom is any one person to blame for the divorce. Usually there are several complex reasons a relationship becomes unsatisfactory. It is better to accept responsibility for your own happiness than to consume your energy in negative behavior and blaming your spouse or yourself. Easy, right? No, it is not easy. You may have to complete grieving before you can begin healing and initiating more positive responses.

In the meantime, place the following message on your bathroom mirror (refrigerator door or car visor) as a reminder, or say it to yourself every morning and as many times a day as you need in order to own it. **"My happiness depends solely on me. I alone have the power to create it."**

BIBLIOGRAPHY

DIVORCE and BEYOND

The Good Divorce. Constance Ahrons, Ph.D., New York: HarperPerennial, 1994. Keeping your family together when your marriage falls apart. Strongly recommended.

Learning from Divorce. Robert LaCrosse and Christie Coates, New York: Jossey-Bass, 2003.

Crazy Time: Surviving Divorce. Abrigal Trafford, New York: HarperPerennial, 1992. A step-by-step guide to understanding the predictable emotional passages of men and women after a marriage ends.

Fresh Starts: Men & Women After Divorce. Elizabeth Cauhape, New York: Basic Books, Inc., 1983. Good description of patterns of adaptation after divorce (particularly at mid-life) and the ways people used this crisis as a springboard to growth.

Living Your Best Life. Laura Berman, New York: Fortgang, Tarcher/Putnam, 2001. "Ten strategies for getting from where you are to where you're meant to be."

Nonviolent Communication: A Language of Life. Marshall Rosenberg, Ph.D., Del Mar, CA: Puddle Dancer Press, 1999. Order from CNVC, P. O. Box 2662, Sherman, Texas 75091. Telephone 1-800-255-7696. A wonderful approach to communication from the heart that can promote a more peaceful self.

Surviving the Break-Up: How Children and Parents Cope with Divorce. Judith Wallerstein, Ph.D. and Joan Kelly, Ph.D., New

York: Basic Books, Inc., 1980. A classic that is still valid in discussing the problems of children being raised by single parents.

Necessary Losses. Judith Viorst, New York: Ballantine Books, a division of Random House, Inc., 1986. "The Loves, Illusions, Dependencies and Impossible Expectations That All of Us Have to Give Up in Order to Grow."

The Shelter of Each Other: Rebuilding Our Families. Mary Pipher, Ph.D., New York: Ballantine Books, a division of Random House, Inc., 1996. "A canny mix of optimism and practicality gives Pipher's fans a way to resist the worst of the culture around them and substitute the best of themselves." *Newsweek.*

The Anatomy of Hope. Jerome Groopman, (Harvard Medical School Professor) New York, Random House, 2004. "An inspiring and profoundly enlightening exploration of one doctor's discovery of how hope can change the course of illness."

The Power of Now. Eckhart Tolle, Novalo, CA: New World Library, 2001. "...a reminder to be truly present in our own lives and liberated from our past and future. It can transform your thinking." *O: The Oprah Magazine*

Uncoupling: Turning Points in Intimate Relationships. Diane Vaughan, New York: Vintage Publishing, reprt., 1990

Secrets of Attraction: The Universal Law of Love, Sex and Romance. Sandra Anne Taylor, Carlsbad, CA: Hayhouse, 2001.

PARENTING and CO-PARENTING

Mom's House, Dad's House. Isolina Ricci, Ph.D., New York: MacMillan Publishing Company, {1998} 1980. Making shared custody work: How parents can make two homes for their children after divorce. Strongly recommended.

Helping Your Kids Cope with Divorce the Sandcastles Way. M. Gary Neuman and Patricia Romanoksi, New York: Random House, [1999], 1998. This book is based on the nationally renowned "Sandcastles" workshop.

The Truth About Children and Divorce: Dealing with the Emotions So You and Your Children Can Thrive. Robert E. Emery, Ph.D., London, England: Penguin Books, 2004.

Caught in the Middle. Carla B. Garrity, Toronto: Maxwell Macmillan International, 1997. Protecting the children of high-conflict divorce.

Sharing the Children. Robert E. Adler, Ph.D., Bethesda, MD: Adler & Adler, 1988. Step-by-Step guide to negotiating divorce so your children do not suffer.

Divorce Book for Parents. Vicki Lansky, Deephaven, MN: Book Peddlers, 1996. Focuses on children's reactions to divorce and parenting issues.

For the Sake of the Children. Kris Kline and Stephen Pew, Rocklin, CA: Prima Publishing, 1991. Discusses how to share your children with your ex-spouse despite your anger.

***The Divorced Dad Dilemma*.** Gerald S. Mayer, Ph.D., Phoenix, AZ: Desert City Press, 1994. A father's guide to understanding, grieving and growing beyond the losses of divorce and to developing a deeper, ongoing relationship with his children.

The Nurturing Father. Pruett, New York: Warner Books, 1987. Describes the benefits to everyone and pleasures for everyone of fathers' deepened involvement with their children. Becoming a classic. Also discusses fathers as primary caregivers.

The Divorced Dad's Survival Book. David Knox and K. Leggett, Reading, MA: Perseus Books, 2000. How to stay connected with your kids.

Helping Your Child Succeed After Divorce. Florence Bienenfeld, Ph.D., Claremont, CA: Hunter House, Inc., 1980. Practical ways for divorced parents to work together to do their best for their children.

Parents Are Forever. Shirley A. Thomas, PhD., Springboard Publications, 2003. A Step-by-Step Guide to Becoming Successful Co-Parents After Divorce.

Helping Children Cope with Divorce. Edward Teyber, San Francisco, CA: Jossey-Bass, 2001. What to do and what not to do to make divorce as painless as possible for children.

The Dance of Defiance. Nancy A. Hagener, Scottsdale, Arizona: Shamrock Books, 2005. This is the story of the journey of a mother and son with oppositional defiant disorder. It provides heartfelt understanding of difficult behavior due to the nature of the child as distinct from reactive behavior due to divorce or other traumas in the child's life.

FOR THE CHILDREN

Dinosaurs Divorce: A Guide for Changing Families. M. Brown and L. Brown, Boston, MA: Little, Brown & Company, 1986. (Ages 4-8).

How to Survive Your Parent's Divorce: Kids Advice to Kids. Gaye Kimball, Chico, CA: Equality Press, 1994. Easy-to-read, one-of-a-kind guide for young people and their parents as they reshape their lives post-divorce.

It's Not Your Fault, Koko Bear. Vicki Lansky, 1998. Minnetonka, MN: Book Peddlers; Book trade distribution by Publishers Group West. Koko bear can help children understand divorce and sends a good message.

It's Not the End of the World. Judy Blume, Yearling Books, 1986 (Girls, Ages 9-12).

The Divorce Express. Paula Danziger, New York: Penguin Putnam Books for Young Readers, 1982. Resentful of her parents' divorce, a young girl tries to accommodate herself to their new lives and also find a place for herself.

Amber Brown Sees Red. Paula Danziger, New York: Scholastic Inc., 1997. Amber's mother is engaged to another man and Amber's life is about to change in a big way.

My Mother's House, My Father's House. Judith Vigna, New York: Atheneum, 1989. A child describes having two different houses in which to live, and what it's like to travel back and forth between them. (Preschool-Grade 3).

NOTES

NOTES